HURRICANE

WITHDRAWN

HURRICANE
Faith McNulty

Drawings by Gail Owens

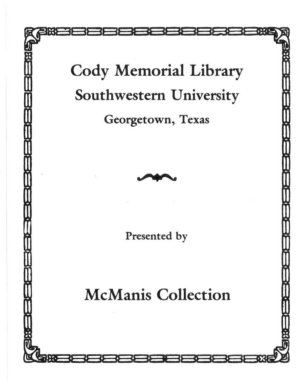
Harper & Row, Publishers

Hurricane

Text copyright © 1983 by Faith McNulty
Illustrations copyright © 1983 by Gail Owens
All rights reserved. No part of this book may be
used or reproduced in any manner whatsoever without
written permission except in the case of brief quotations
embodied in critical articles and reviews. Printed in
the United States of America. For information address
Harper & Row, Publishers, Inc., 10 East 53rd Street,
New York, N.Y. 10022. Published simultaneously in
Canada by Fitzhenry & Whiteside Limited, Toronto.
First Edition

Library of Congress Cataloging in Publication Data
McNulty, Faith.
    Hurricane.

    Summary: John and his family prepare for and
experience a hurricane on the East Coast.
    [1. Hurricanes—Fiction] I. Owens, Gail, ill.
II. Title.
PZ7.M4788Hu 1983   [E]   79-2672
ISBN 0-06-024142-X   AACR2
ISBN 0-06-024143-8 (lib. bdg.)

To Johnny

1

John woke thinking of the hurricane—the hurricane and the big tree.

For several days the weatherman had warned that a hurricane was coming toward the New England shore. This was the day it might strike. If it did, there was danger that the huge tree that stood beside the old farmhouse might fall.

John went down to the kitchen. His mother and dad were listening to the radio. "What's happening?" John asked. "Is it coming today?"

"Nobody knows," his father said. "During the night it picked up speed. It's headed our way. But it still could turn and blow out to sea."

John glanced at the windows. White mist pressed against the panes. Already the day seemed strange. The air felt hot and stale. John went outside and looked up at the big tree.

The tree was so tall that its top branches were lost in the fog. John could barely see the platform of his tree house in the first big fork of the giant tree. He went to a ladder nailed to the trunk and began to climb. There was a bark from below. As usual, Goldy, his little yellow dog, wanted to come up, too. John climbed down and picked her up. She was a small dog and he was able to carry her tucked under one arm. He needed only one free hand to climb.

John lay down on the platform and looked into the branches that went up and up into the clouds. He remembered the summer days two years ago when his dad had helped him build the tree house. The first time John had climbed up and looked down at the ground his stomach had taken him by surprise . . . as though he had swallowed ice. Soon he had grown accustomed to seeing the ground so far below.

John and his dad had built a platform in a crotch in the tree, pulling up the planks with a rope, one by one. This summer John had built another ladder to an even higher branch . . . and then to another. But still he was nowhere near the top. Still the trunk of the tree was so big that his outstretched arms could reach only partway around.

The tree house had no roof except the branches and leaves above, but to John it felt like a house. He liked to sit there and think—or read—or write in his diary—or lie on his back and look into the branches as he was doing now. One hot summer night he had gone up in darkness and watched fireflies and stars and seen the moon rise.

John kept some books and his diary in a large wooden box. He opened the box now and took out his diary. There was a page for each day. He turned to September third and wrote: "There is a hurricane coming. It is somewhere out at sea. I hope it doesn't hit here. By this time tomorrow I will know." He started to close the book and then added a line: "It will be awful if it knocks down this tree!"

John heard his mother calling him. He put the diary back in the box. He picked up Goldy and carried her down the ladder.

His mother and dad were having breakfast. John sat down to a plate of scrambled eggs.

"Dad," he asked, "why is a hurricane different from other storms? What makes it worse?"

"The wind is much stronger," his dad said. "Hurricanes form out over the sea. The wind starts to blow in a huge circle. It is like a doughnut of whirling air."

"If the air is going in a circle, why doesn't it just stay in one place?"

"Have you seen a top spin? It spins and at the same time it moves along on the floor. That's what a hurricane does. The wind in a hurricane is spinning and the whole hurricane is moving slowly over the sea."

"How strong is the wind?"

"Over seventy-five miles an hour. Sometimes a hundred miles an hour or even more."

"Do they come often?"

"At this time of year—at the end of summer—quite a few hurricanes build up in the south Atlantic. Most of them blow themselves out over the water. But sometimes one will turn toward land. Then it can cause trouble to people in its path."

"What happens when it hits?"

"Well, usually the lights go out. Along beaches, the waves get huge and the water rises. Sometimes shore roads are flooded and beach houses washed away."

"Could this house get washed away?"

"No. We're safe—high on this bluff. But I guess we could lose the roof—in a really big storm."

"Or the big tree?"

John's father nodded. His mother said, "I couldn't bear it if we lost the tree."

"Why won't the lights work in a hurricane?" John asked.

"Because the wind blows down the wires—or branches fall across them and break them."

"What happens then?"

"The refrigerator won't work. The electric stove won't work. The gas station can't pump gas. All sorts of things won't work."

"Don't worry, John," his mother said. "We can get along without those things. It will be like old times, before people had electricity. We can live in this house the way the people who built it lived in it a hundred years ago."

His dad said, "Well, let's get started. There's a lot to do. If the storm comes we'll be ready for it."

"What can we do?"

"Get wood for the old black iron stove—oil for the lamp. Get candles."

His mother said, "I'm making a list."

"The first thing I'm going to do," his father said, "is make sure the boat is okay. Come on, John, I need your help."

John and his father went out and walked down the path between bayberry bushes. Goldy trotted at John's heels. They reached the cliff above the cove where their small sailboat rode at anchor. For a moment they stood and looked out across the water. The air was calm. The sea and the sky were pale

gray. The fog had lifted, but clouds hung low. They were ordinary clouds, but somehow everything seemed a little different—a little strange.

Their boat—the *Scallop Shell*—was rocking as small waves hit her sides with gentle slaps. Their dinghy—the *Barnacle*—lay turned over on the sand. John and his dad climbed down the steep path to the beach. They picked up the dinghy and carried her to the water. John's dad got in and took the oars.

John picked up Goldy and shoved off the boat. When it was afloat, he jumped into the stern. Ahead he could see the sandbars that protected their cove. Beyond the sandbars lay the open ocean.

"Hey, Dad," he said. "I hear a thundering sound."

"The surf is building up," his dad said. "The waves from the hurricane reach shore ahead of the wind. Later let's go down to the open beach and have a look. It's fun to watch a big surf."

"Will the surf come in here, where we are?"

"No. The waves will break on the sandbar out there. That's why this cove is a safe place for little boats. But the tide may rise very high."

They reached the *Scallop Shell.* John's dad held the dinghy close to the bigger boat while John jumped onto her deck. "Make her fast," his dad said. "Tie the painter to the forward cleat." He tossed John a rope. John caught it neatly and twisted it around the cleat in a half hitch.

John's dad climbed aboard and unfastened the sails. He and John stuffed them into canvas bags and stowed them in the cabin below. They took turns pumping out water that had collected under the floorboards. John's father threw out a second anchor, mooring the *Scallop Shell* more securely. He checked the fastenings on the portholes and told John to bring all the seat cushions into the cabin.

Finally John's dad put a wooden hatch cover over the top of the cabin and closed the metal fasteners that held it in place. "That's what sailors call 'battening the hatches,'" he said. "Now our little *Scallop Shell* should ride out any storm."

They got back into the *Barnacle.* Goldy had been sitting in the dinghy alone, waiting, watching everything John did. She licked his face and leaned against him, glad he had returned. As his dad rowed toward the shore, John noticed sea gulls flying high. They were flying inland, away from the ocean. The sky had turned darker and their white wings gleamed against the dull gray.

"Dad? Do the gulls know a hurricane is coming?"

"I think they do," his dad said. "When a hurricane is coming, there are changes in the air. We use instruments—such as a barometer—to measure the changes. It is possible that birds feel weather changes in their bones—or sense them in some other way we don't know about."

They were nearing the beach. John looked up at the sandy cliff and saw that the yellow beach grass at the edge was bending a little as small gusts of wind swept over it. He could see their house, and his mother taking their bathing suits off the clothesline—and the big tree standing like a tower, so tall that it made their house look small.

"Dad. My tree house. What will happen to it? Do you think it will be blown away?"

"It might be." His father, busy with the oars, seemed to be thinking of more important things.

"Dad, how about the big tree? How much wind would it take to blow it down?"

"It depends," his father said. "It depends on how the wind hits it and how deep the roots are. That tree has lived through many hurricanes, but it is bigger now, and so it is more likely to be blown down."

"Why?"

"Because there is more surface for the wind to push against. Someday it will have to go, but I hope I won't be here to see it fall."

"How old do you think the tree is?"

"I don't know. Very old."

The *Barnacle* touched the beach. John and his father carried it to high ground and turned it over with the oars underneath. John was still thinking about the tree. It seemed terrible that something so huge and grand might be overthrown.

"Try to guess how old it is," he asked.

"Over two hundred years, I'm sure," his father said.

John subtracted two hundred years from nineteen hundred and eighty-two. "Then George Washington was alive when the tree began to grow," he said. "Probably there were Indians camping on this beach."

John ran up the cliff path to the house. His mother was in the yard. She said, "Please pick up everything lying around that might blow away or blow against a window and break it." She was gathering clothespins from the ground. His dad began to put the garden tools in the shed.

When the yard was tidy, his mother said, "I think you'd better go to town and get a few things. I'd like to have plenty of food in the house in case we can't get to the store for a few days."

2

"Let's go, John," his father said, and got into their old station wagon. John and Goldy got in beside him. Their first stop was the hardware store. People were lined up at the counter. There was a handwritten sign nailed up: "Only two candles to a customer. Only two flashlight batteries." Behind the counter Mrs. Jones was busy filling orders.

The people waiting their turn were all talking about the hurricane. "Looks like we're going to get it, sure enough," a woman said.

"You can't tell," a man answered. "If you get ready, then it's more than likely to turn out to sea. If you don't get ready, then it will hit—sure as shootin'."

An old man who looked like a fisherman was talking to another. He said the worst hurricane he could remember was in 1938—over forty years ago. "Darn near every boat in the harbor was smashed, or piled up on the beach. The waves

picked some up and set them down on the roofs of houses."

"We didn't have any warning in those days," the other old man said. "Hurricanes just came out of a blue sky."

The fisherman said, "In 1938 there were summer houses out on the sand spit. The waves carried them away like matchboxes. It was lucky it was late in the year and the summer people had gone home. Except for one fellow. He forgot his cat. He came back to get it, and while he was there the water washed up into the house. The man climbed onto the roof. Then the house broke loose. The man and his cat floated around on that roof all night long. The Coast Guard picked them up the next day."

A woman said, "I heard on the radio that there's a Coast Guard plane up there following this hurricane, keeping track of where it is and how strong the winds are."

John's father moved to the counter as his turn came. He bought two candles, two flashlight batteries, a roll of tape and a gallon of kerosene.

"You're on high ground on that cliff," Mrs. Jones said. "You don't have to worry about water in your cellar."

"That's right," John's father said. "Our house is strong. It's been through a lot of hurricanes in its time. We're not worried. Are we, John?" He smiled down at John, who was gathering up the packages. John shrugged. He didn't know what his feelings were. There was excitement and there was also fear.

His father and Mrs. Jones wished each other luck and said good-bye. The next stop was the grocery store. Again there was a line of people waiting. John's mother had made out a list of food they could keep without a refrigerator—powdered milk, cheese, carrots, apples, eggs, onions, canned soup, peanut butter and bread.

When the bags were stowed in the car John's father looked at his watch. "I think we have time to go down and see the ocean," he said. He turned the car onto the road that led to the shore and the open sea.

As they neared the beach the wind grew stronger. The car swayed when gusts struck it. His father parked near the break-water. As John got out, wind hit him in the face. It tasted salty on his lips. Fine sand stung his face and made tears come to his eyes. All summer John and his parents had swum here in gentle surf, diving and playing in slow, lazy waves. Now the waves were huge, racing each other to the beach. Each wave reared up higher than the last and surged in at terrific speed, chasing the one ahead. As wave followed wave, each crashed in turn, foamed up on the sand, then sank back to be swallowed by the wave behind.

This was a different sea from any John had ever seen.

"My gosh," his father said, "those waves are a beautiful sight. I've never seen them this high. Look! There's a fishing boat heading for port. They must be having a rough time out there."

Far out John could see a boat rising on the crests and then sinking almost out of sight as it dipped into the troughs between the waves. White foam splashed at the bow. The boat looked very small as it struggled in the heavy sea. Finally it made its way around the end of the breakwater into the shelter of the cove.

"We'd better get home," his father said. "There's still lots to do."

At home his father went to work putting strips of tape across the windowpanes. He explained that if something driven by the wind hit a pane, the tape would keep the glass from shattering into little pieces.

John was given his share of things to do. He washed old cider jugs and filled them with clean drinking water. He gathered dry wood and brought it into the kitchen.

"Isn't it lucky," his mother said, "that we never threw out the old black iron stove!" She was busy cleaning the refrigerator. "These things won't keep without electricity. We'll have a feast for lunch—chicken, salad, and ice cream with raspberries."

While they feasted they listened to the radio. The weather report said the same things over and over. The hurricane was moving toward them . . . it probably would hit their shore early that night. People were advised to leave the beaches . . . to haul in boats . . . not to leave cars parked under trees . . . to fill bottles with clean drinking water. There was a long list.

While they ate and listened, John stared out the window. Everything looked so normal, it was hard to believe that by tomorrow the storm might have changed everything—blown down trees, perhaps even torn off the roof.

His mother must have been reading his mind. She said, "I'm not going to worry. This house has been here a hundred years or more. It must have lived through many, many storms and it will live through this one. I don't want you to worry either, John."

John still found he could not visualize such a storm. How could there be a force so strong? "Dad, can you *see* a hurricane?" he asked.

"I've seen photographs of hurricanes taken from airplanes flying above them," his father said. "A hurricane isn't solid, of course. It is made up of fog and rain. The whirling winds suck up water from the ocean, and that becomes rain. In a photograph the storm looks like a huge, dark wheel—sort of ragged at the edges."

"Isn't there some way to *stop* a hurricane?" John asked. He had always thought of human beings as being able to control almost anything.

His father said, "I've heard talk about scientists looking for ways to break up big storms or change their direction. But so far no one knows how to do it. There are still some things too big for us to tackle."

His mother said, "I'm not sure I want anyone to invent a way to change hurricanes and storms. People have lived with storms for millions of years. It is a part of living. We seem to think of natural things as good or bad depending on what effect they have on our own lives. But it seems to me we should think of nature as a whole. Perhaps storms make changes that are good in ways we don't know about—that are necessary to keep everything in balance."

John found it hard to imagine good coming from a storm that could do so much damage. "What about boats and houses that are smashed?" he asked. "And people getting killed?"

"Boats and houses can be built again," his mother said. "And now that we have warning of coming storms there is less danger that people will be hurt. I think learning to live with nature is better than trying to change it."

"What about trees?" John asked. "What about our big tree? Isn't there some way we can protect it?"

His father smiled and shook his head.

"It will have to go someday," John's mother said. "All living things do. A hurricane that blows down old trees makes room for seedlings to grow."

"Dad?" John asked. "Do you think it would do any good to tie down my tree house?"

"Maybe," his father said. "There's plenty of rope in the barn."

John went out to the barn. Goldy followed closely at his heels. All day she had become more and more anxious—staying close to his side and watching every move he made. There was no doubt she sensed that there was danger on the way. John took the rope and climbed the ladder. Goldy, at the bottom of the tree, whined and begged. "Not this time, Goldy," John said. "I'll be down in a minute."

John lashed the platform to the branches as best he could. Then, on an impulse, he climbed to the branch above and then to the one above that. He sat astride it and looked out toward the ocean.

From this great height John could see the cove and the *Scallop Shell* at anchor. He could see the sandbar at the far-off shore. There were bursts of white foam as waves crashed on the beach. The booming sound of the surf came clearly to his ears.

Wind touched his face lightly and the leaves around him rustled. The grass in the meadow swayed in smooth waves. He heard the thin, faraway voices of sea gulls. Looking up, he saw them soaring inland and imagined they had seen the

hurricane and were crying, "Flyaway. . . . Flyaway. . . . Fly-away. . . ."

For some reason the dread that had been growing inside him all day lifted. Suddenly John felt that he and the gulls—the tree—even the distant ocean waves—were all linked together in a way he had never realized before. Each was responding to the coming storm. Each would meet it in its own way.

3

Rain drops pattered on the leaves around him. John scrambled down to the platform. The sky had become very dark. He hastily took his diary and books and climbed to the ground. He stood there for a moment looking up into the sky. The rain was warm—warmer than the air. And the wind was rising in strength. Soft gusts breathed through the leaves. Then stronger currents made the branches bend and sway. With his books tucked under his arm John ran to the house.

"Hey, Mom," he said. "I think it's begun. I think the hurricane is coming now."

"I think so, too," his mother said.

John went to his room and changed his wet clothes. The rain drummed on the roof and poured down the windowpanes in sheets.

When he returned to the kitchen—Goldy still at his heels—his parents were at the table listening to the radio. The weather-

man was reporting that the storm had already crossed parts of Long Island. Some streets were flooded. Some highways were blocked by fallen trees. Electricity had been shut off in many places. But because of careful preparations no one had been hurt. Now the storm was sweeping up the coast. It was still gathering speed.

John's father turned off the radio. "We've done everything we can," he said. "And I think we're going to be all right." He picked up a book and sat down to read.

John's mother said, "I think I'll iron some clothes. Tomorrow the electric iron probably won't work." She set up the ironing board. A moment later the lights went out. "Too late," she said, and put the iron down.

John's father closed his book. "I'll light the lamps," he said.

Until the light failed, John hadn't realized that evening had come. Now he saw that it was almost dark outside. The window-panes were blue-gray. Inside the kitchen he could barely see his mother and father, the table, the stove. How strange the room looked in a light that was neither daylight nor dark. His father struck a match. An oil lamp glowed in the center of the table. The light was a warm, golden color.

"Believe it nor not," his father said, "Abraham Lincoln studied his law books by a lamp like that."

"When this house was built," his mother said, "the family must have spent every evening by lamplight. There was no radio; no television. They sewed and talked and read aloud."

His mother had started a fire in the stove. She put the kettle

on and laid out a light supper—bread and cheese, apples and hot cocoa. The noise of the storm was growing. The drumming of the rain and the roar of the wind mingled in one huge noise. Leaves and twigs hit the windowpanes. The walls of the house trembled in the bigger gusts.

By the time they had finished eating, the noise had become as loud as thunder—as loud as an express train rushing past a station. Goldy had crept under the table. Quivering, she pressed against his leg. John himself felt a cold lump of fear and excitement gathering inside him. He hoped his parents wouldn't guess that he was afraid.

"This must be the peak of the storm," John's father said. "If the house can stand this it can stand anything." His voice was very calm.

"What about the tree?" John asked. "Would we hear it go down?"

"I doubt it," his father said. "Not in this noise."

John went to the window that faced the big tree, but he could see nothing but blackness outside. "I wish I could see the tree," he said. "Do you think we could go out and look? Maybe just open the door a crack?"

"No," his mother said. "If you open the door you might not be able to pull it shut again."

"Wait a few minutes," his father said. "I think the wind is dropping. This may be the eye of the storm." He explained that in the center of the storm—the hole in the doughnut—there is a calm place. While it passed over them there would be no wind. Then, as the other side of the wheel of wind arrived, there would again be hurricane winds. These would blow in the opposite direction from the winds in the first part of the storm.

Within a few minutes the fury of the wind lessened. The sound dropped from a shriek to a moan to a whisper. "Come on," his father said. "Let's have a look." He took his rain gear off a hook and handed John his yellow slicker. Then, carefully, he opened the door. Warm, wet air pressed against them. They slipped out and slammed the door behind them. They stood in the darkness sheltered by the roof of the porch.

There was a faint glow of light in the western sky. John could see the outline of the big tree—could see that it still stood. "Oh Dad," John said, "I'm so glad!"

"So am I," his father said, "but we still have the second half of the storm to live through."

They stood in the darkness for several minutes. After so much noise and turmoil the silence and calm were strange. John noticed that the air was fragrant with the smell of crushed leaves.

Then the wind began to rise again. It came quickly. John could see the branches of the big tree begin to sway—then toss and bend. Leaves were torn from the branches and whirled into the sky.

"Hey," his father said. "We'd better get back inside."

"Wait a minute," John said. "Just a minute more." The wind was coming from the side of the house opposite the porch, and though it shrieked around the corners of the house, John and his father were sheltered. John felt the danger of the storm

close to them and at the same time the safety of the lamplit room just inside the door.

A tremendous gust hit the big tree. It seemed to bend almost double before the wind. Its branches writhed. A limb snapped with a sound like a pistol shot and was carried away into the blackness. Rain began to fall again. By the light from the window John could see that it was falling in streams that slanted like jets from a shower.

"Dad," John said. "I think this is worse than before. Do you think the tree can stand it?"

"I don't know," his father said. "But I know we've got to get inside."

A gust of wind whirled around the corner and rocked John back on his heels. There was a ripping, tearing sound; a crash.

"I think the tool shed blew over," his father shouted.

"The tree!" John shouted back. "What about the tree?" Gusts of wind hit his face and seemed to tear the breath from his lips. . . . Again the noise was deafening. The light had vanished. He could see nothing in the blackness. He knew the tree was fighting for its life. His heart beat fast as he thought of its struggle. He had never felt so small. Because there was nothing else he could do, he said silently, "Good luck, tree. Bless you, tree. Do your best."

His father had opened the door. He grabbed John's arm and pulled him inside. The door slammed behind them. John stood, blinking in the lamplight. He felt dazed by the power of the storm.

"What happened?" his mother asked. "I heard a crash."

"It's pretty exciting out there," his father said. "I think we may be minus a tool shed."

"And the big tree?" his mother asked.

"It's losing a lot of leaves," his father said, "and some branches, too. But it's still standing."

"You both look wet," his mother said. "We might as well all go to bed." She went up the stairs holding the lamp. John and his father followed. She put the lamp in the bathroom for John to undress by and gave him a flashlight to light his way to bed.

Goldy followed him. Usually she slept in the kitchen, but tonight everything was different. When John got into bed she jumped up too. She nestled beside him and John could feel her whole body trembling. "Don't worry, Goldy," he murmured, stroking her. Comforting her, John felt less afraid. He expected to stay awake—listening as the waves of wind surged over the roof—but somehow he fell asleep.

4

John awoke—suddenly—in darkness. The wind shrieked at the window beside his bed. The panes rattled. The house shivered with each gust. It seemed that in another moment the roof above him would be torn away. He sat up in bed, shaking with cold and fear. He reached for the flashlight. A beam of light showed him that the room was unchanged. But the howl of the wind grew even stronger. A great gust struck the house. Then another. Suddenly there was a blast of noise. Then wind struck him and icy water showered him. The window near his bed had shattered as some heavy object, driven by the wind, struck it. Glass crashed to the floor. A shower of rain—as though from a dozen hoses—was soaking his bed. Gusts of wind were sweeping into the room. A picture fell off the wall and a rocking chair began to rock.

John leaped from bed and ran into the hall, slamming the door behind him. In the beam of his flashlight he saw his father.

"What happened? Are you all right?"

"The window broke."

John's teeth were chattering. His pajamas were wet with rain.

"Thank God that's all," his father said. "I thought it was the roof. It made such a crash."

"What are you going to do?" John asked.

"Get some plywood," his father said. "There's some in the cellar."

John's mother appeared, holding the lamp. His father told her what had happened. He took the flashlight and went to the cellar. His mother said, "John, you're soaked. I'll get you some dry pajamas." He held the lamp while she searched a laundry basket in the bathroom. When he had changed she rubbed his wet hair with a towel. Then he dried off Goldy, who was wet and shivering, too.

His father came up the stairs carrying the plywood and tools. He opened the door to John's room. Wind and rain were pouring through the empty window. The curtain flapped. But the sound of the storm was no longer quite so loud. John held the lamp while his father nailed the plywood over the window. As soon as it was in place the room was calm and snug again.

"Your bed is too wet to sleep in," his father said. "Get your sleeping bag and come in with your mother and me."

John found the bag in the closet and followed his father. His mother had gone back to bed. "Is everything okay?" she asked sleepily from the darkness.

"Everything's okay," his father said. "The storm is about over, too."

John unrolled his sleeping bag on the floor and crawled into it. The wind had died down to a soft whine. It was a gentle, lullaby sound. Goldy lay beside him—a warm, solid shape— no longer trembling. He heard his father and mother breathing in sleep. He felt very snug, very safe.

Then—suddenly—he thought of the tree. Was it still standing? Please, please, he thought, let the big tree be safe, too.

It was daylight. Sun was shining through the bedroom window. John awoke, surprised to find himself on the floor. Then he remembered why he was there. He glanced at his parents' bed. It was empty. John leaped up and looked out the window. Leaves and branches littered the yard. In the meadow a tall pine tree lay on its side. Its roots had been torn from the earth. The tool shed lay keeled over against a stone wall. What about the big tree? It stood on the other side of the house. John couldn't see it from this window.

He ran down the stairs to the front door. He pulled it open . . . and there was the tree. It stood straight and tall, but changed. Its branches were bare. Every leaf had been blown away. Branches had been torn off. Soggy leaves and broken branches littered the yard.

John went into the kitchen. His mother was frying eggs on the old iron stove.

"Hi," she said. "Aren't we lucky! No damage except the

window and the tool shed. Thank God, the big tree came through."

"It's lost all its leaves," John said.

"That won't hurt it," his mother said. "They would have fallen soon anyway. Next spring new leaves will come just like always."

"What about the branches that blew off?" John asked.

"The tree won't miss them," his mother said. "But I'm afraid your tree house blew away. The pieces are over in the field. Come and sit down."

She put a plate of eggs on the table. John sat down and began to eat. The eggs tasted wonderful. While he ate he tried to remember what had happened during the night. Now, with the sun shining in the windows, the storm seemed unreal, like something he had dreamed; but the signs of its visit, the naked trees, the torn branches, were strewn all over the yard.

Suddenly John felt tremendously happy. He was glad the storm was over—but he wouldn't have missed it for the world. He went out into the yard. The air was sparkling. He looked into the blue sky and saw sea gulls sailing calmly toward the ocean. He heard their thin voices crying, ". . . Safe again. . . . Safe again. . . ." The storm was something he and the gulls—and everything in its path—had survived together. The storm had been real—real and huge and dangerous—but not evil—just a part of the natural world that they all shared.

John looked up into the branches of the big tree and began to plan a new tree house—one he would build next summer. He saw a perfect place for it, higher than he had ever climbed before.

ABOUT THE AUTHOR

Faith McNulty is a well-known nature writer. Her articles on the whooping crane, the black-footed ferret and the great whales, all of which have appeared in The New Yorker, *have been published as books. She has also written several books for young readers, including WOODCHUCK, A Science I CAN READ Book; WHALES: THEIR LIFE IN THE SEA; MOUSE AND TIM; HOW TO DIG A HOLE TO THE OTHER SIDE OF THE WORLD and THE ELEPHANT WHO COULDN'T FORGET.*

ABOUT THE ARTIST

Gail Owens was born in Detroit, Michigan, and now lives in upstate New York. She is the illustrator of numerous books for children, including THE EELS' STRANGE JOURNEY by Judi Friedman, SPIDER IN THE SKY by Anne Rose, FOG IN THE MEADOW by Joanne Ryder and OUT IN THE DARK AND DAYLIGHT by Aileen Fisher.